C000275502

Nature Journal
Seasonal Creative Projects
Published in 2018 by Burt & Wie

ISBN: 978-1-5272-1970-0
Printed by KOPA® www.kopa.eu

www.loveyoursketchbook.com

FSC
www.fsc.org
MIX
Paper from responsible sources
FSC® C103625

Nature Journal

Seasonal Creative Projects

By Zoë Burt & Marianne Wie

YELLOW COSMOS
Cosmos sulphureus
JAPANESE INDIGO
Dyer's Knotweed
Polygonum tinctorium
MADDER
Rubia tinctorum
WELD
Reseda Luteola
GOLDENROD
Solidago
GROW YOUR OWN COLOUR
HOLLYHOCK
Alcea rosea
DAHLIA
Dahlia
DYERS CHAMOMILE
Anthemis tinctoria
WOAD
Isatis tinctoria
ST JOHN'S WORT
Hypericum Perforatum
LADY'S BEDSTRAW
Galium verum
SAW-WORT
Serratula tinctoria

Contents

Foreword: From Digital to *Digitalis*

Nature is all around us, and indeed sustains us at every moment of our lives.

My role at Chelsea Physic Garden is to connect diverse audiences from all walks of life to the wonders of the natural world via the Garden's varied collections – thus continuing a long tradition going back about 350 years where the Worshipful Society of Apothecaries began growing plants there for medicinal use. Nowadays we have the opportunity to demonstrate so many more uses of plants than 'mere' healing.

The great outdoors has, does and always will inspire designers, artists (of all genres), scientists and engineers to devise, design and create new things to make the world a better place – whether they are useful, beautiful or preferably both.

Zoë and Marianne are experts in their fields (literally) and I am sure *Nature Journal* will inspire you to connect to your own environment, nature and the seasons by trying out fun, practical and traditional tried-and-tested techniques and skills which you can then pass on to others – both as knowledge and as unique gifts.

This book is the perfect antidote and companion to life in the digital age and our perceived reliance upon technology – a lovely new spin on a pocket field notebook or nature diary which I'm sure will keep you entertained for years.

Michael Holland FLS, Jan 2018
Head of Education at Chelsea Physic Garden and author of
I Ate Sunshine for Breakfast

March
May
May
Bifora

Invitation

The vision behind this journal is to inspire you to be creative with the projects and recipes in this book, and to connect and enjoy every season in nature. Hopefully this will lead you to new ideas that will transform into your own personal field notes and artwork.

Any pages which have the ink pen and pencil illustrations are for you to add your own thoughts and sketches. Why not squeeze out a used teabag and paint across a page to make an interesting background? Try flicking or dripping some berry juice onto the page to make this seasonal nature journal your own.

We hope this book can inspire collaborative projects between friends and families. For us this journal has been an opportunity to leave the digital world behind and spend creative time outside. We invite you to to do the same.

Love your sketchbook!

Burt & Wie

Spring

YOUR YARN DYEING
Elsie G. Davenport
YOUR YARN DYEING

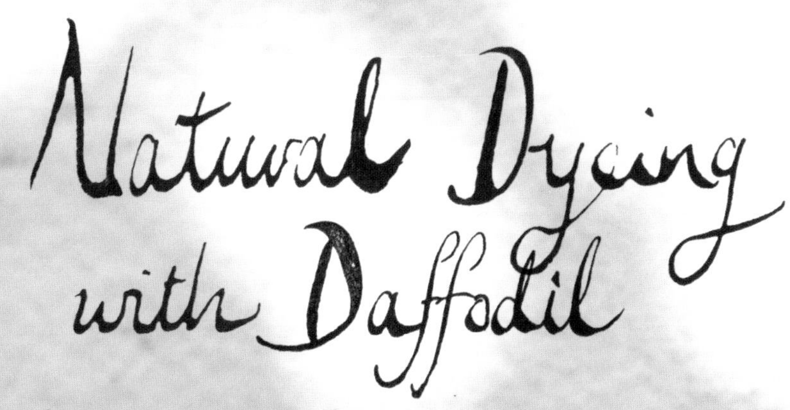

Natural Dyeing with Daffodil

Scientific name: *Narcissus pseudonarcissus*

Native to Europe

Grow from bulbs or purchase cut flowers

After enjoying a vase full of these spring flowers, use dry or fresh petals as a dye for shades of yellow

The bulb contains toxins and the sap can be an irritant, so handle with care

Always use separate utensils and cooking pans to those used for eating

Materials:

- A couple of bunches of daffodil flower heads
- Natural fabric or yarn
- A dye pot (a big old stainless steel pot is ideal)
- Tongs, water and heat source

Method:

Place a bunch of flower heads into the dye pot and cover with water and simmer gently for about half an hour. Do not boil. The petals can be strained through a sieve and the wetted out fibres or yarn added to the dye bath and gently heated for a further half an hour. Stir often for an even dye surface.

Mordanting

– what is it and why do it?

The purpose of mordanting fabric is to help the fabric receive the colour, intensify the colour and aid wash and lightfastness. There are various mordants in the form of salt compounds, the most common being alum which has been used by dyers for centuries. See page 91 for the recipe.

When to mordant?

This can be done before dyeing or added to the dye bath for an all-in-one method or mordanting can take place after dyeing, which can result in exciting colour changes – see note below on expanding the colour palette. Some dyers use their pots as mordants. For example, aluminium, iron and copper.

Some plant dyes do not need a mordant and include onion skins, dried buddleia flower heads, and the bark of tannin rich trees.

Natural mordants

These can be found in bramble stems and leaves, staghorn sumac leaves which both contain tannin, rhubarb leaves which contain oxalic acid, and alum rich leaves such as symplocos. Around the world people have discovered other plants to help in this process such as lemon grass and tamarind.

Record dry weights of natural mordant materials and fibres to develop knowledge and experience.

The colours from these natural mordants will also bring a range of new hues as the tannin rich plants give a light tan base and rhubarb leaves yield a yellow shade.

Expanding the colour palette:

An after bath of iron water solution (to modify colour) will turn the colour green. See page 59 for instructions.

Notes:

Soaking flower heads prior to dying can produce richer shades of yellow.

Natural fibres accept dyes differently. Wool and silk will absorb the colour more readily than cellulose fibres which come from plants such as cotton or linen.

Contact Printing with Botanicals

This is a simple way to release pigments from plants. Choose a selection of petals, flowers or leaves. Some plants work better than others. Violets and nasturtiums print well as do any petals with extra stripey markings.

Materials:

- Scissors
- Masking tape
- Sketchbook or paper
- Flowers or leaves

Method:

Place plant matter face down on to fabric or paper. Masking tape can be used to secure botancial matter and prevent movement.

Use a pebble or small hammer to tap out the edges of the plant. You can watch the colour coming through and adjust pressure accordingly.

Try different fabric bases such as cotton, hemp, linen, silk and weaves for varied results. Make notes on seasons and plant names to broaden your knowledge of this print process.

Use lemon juice to create petal colour changes on the purple, red and blue spectrum. Painting with iron water solution also creates darker marks.

Note:
These ephemeral prints will fade in sunlight over time, but will keep their colour inside a book.

Herbarium specimen

A herbarium specimen is all parts of the plant preserved for scientific study. To dry the plant, you need to remove moisture to prevent mould forming.

How to press plants

- Choose plants to preserve.
- Use sharp scissors or secateurs to cut plants.
- Lay them in between absorbent sheets of paper.
- Press them in a flower press or between pages of a heavy book and leave for three days to a couple of weeks.

To develop plant knowledge, add notes like:

Name: note the common name of the plant and the scientific name.

Location: where did the plant come from?

Date: what season or date was it picked?

Characteristics: leaf shapes, number of petals? Describe the plant.

Properties: does the plant have any medicinal, culinary or colour-giving properties?

Lantana camara

- Collected in Nisyros, Greece.
- Also known as wild sage.
- A flowering plant within the verbena family.
- Attracts butterflies and birds.
- After pollination the tubular flowers change colour.
- The berry turns from green to dark purple.
- Used in traditional medicine.

SLBI
Garden or Opium Poppy
Papaver somniferum L.
HERB.—A. O. HUME.
ORDER
GENUS
SPECIES
VAR.
COUNTY Kent PLACE
Collected by
Date
7608.

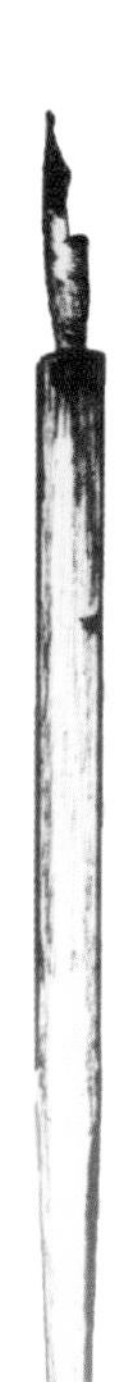

Summer

Stitch a herbarium specimen

You will need:

Inspiration from your own pressed flowers or a herbarium specimen to create a design.

Materials:

- Carbon paper or vanishing fabric marker
- Pencil
- Fabric
- Embroidery hoop
- Embroidery threads
- Embroidery needle
- Scissors

Method:

Lightly freestyle draw with a vanishing pen, copying from your pressed plant on to a chosen fabric. Or use carbon paper to trace face down on fabric from a printed out herbarium sheet. Press firmly down with a pencil to transfer your design.

Use this carbon transfer as a basis for your stitch design.

Choose embroidery threads or dye your own using botanical dyes.

Here are some stitch ideas to help you get going. Practise a few on a scrap of fabric.

Couching – thread is laid across the fabric and secured with small stitches in self or contrast colour

Back Stitch

draw a stitch line & take a backward stitch bring needle through in front + take another backward stitch

French Knot

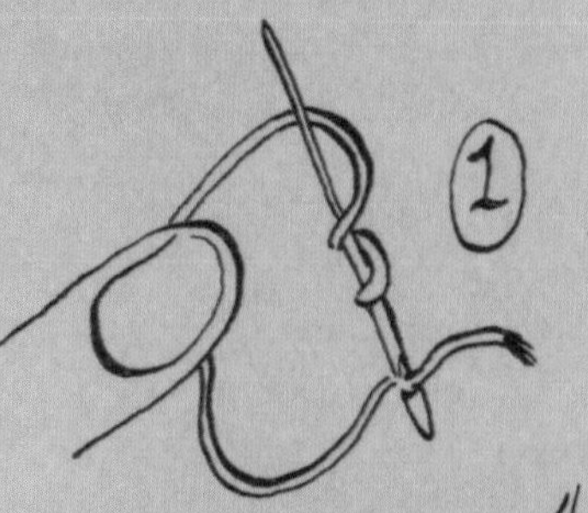

1. Loop thread around needle 2-3 times
2. Keep tension on thread as knots are secured at fabric surface
3.

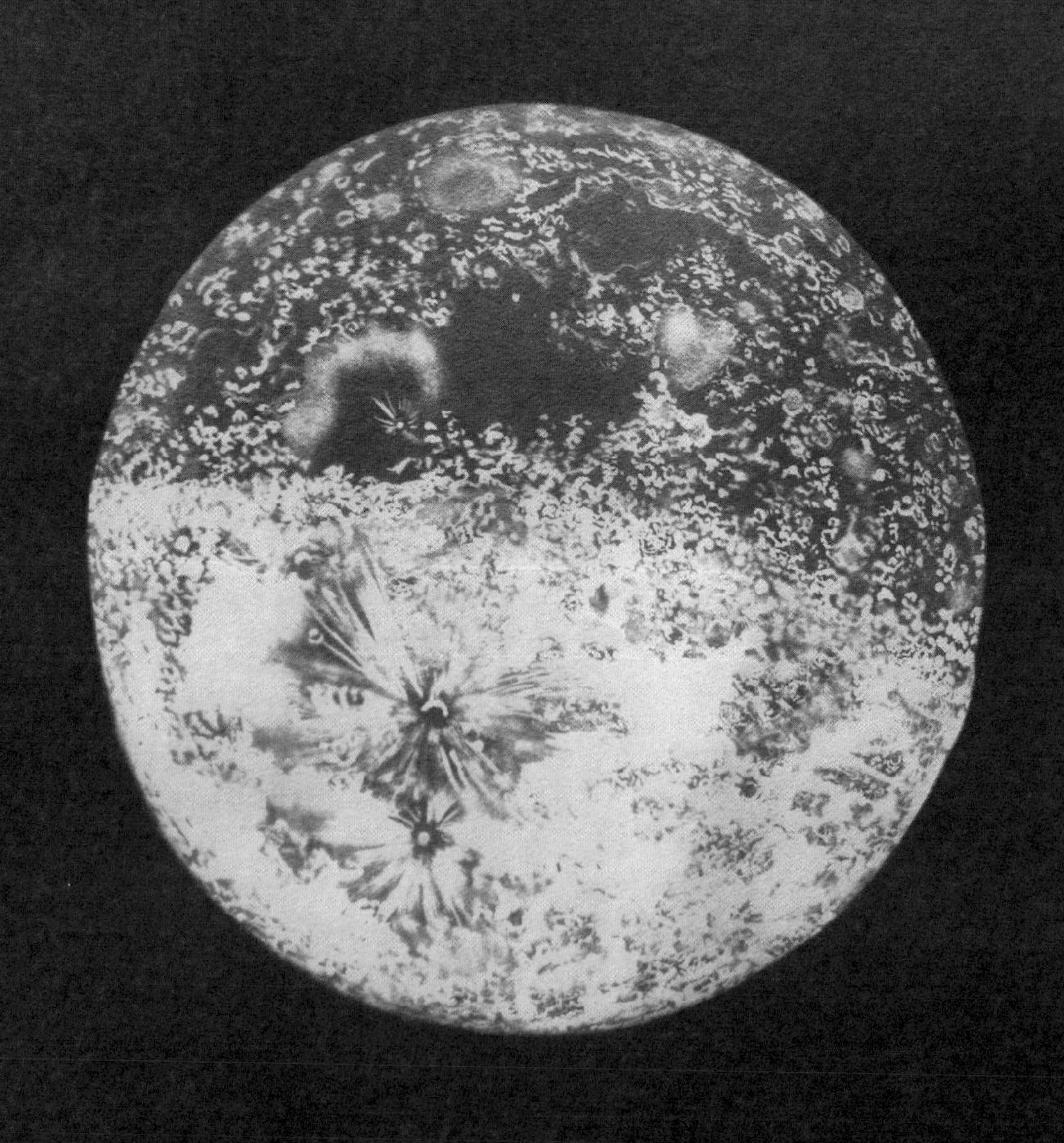

Blueprint

Cyanotype

– also known as blueprinting or sunprinting

This process was invented in 1842 by Sir John Herschel, who was a renowned scientist, astronomer, mathematician, inventor and early photographer.

The botanist Anna Atkins became one of the pioneers of this technique. She made three volumes of books documenting British algae between 1843 and 1853 using the cyanotype process. Only 17 copies of the book are known to exist. Copies are held at The British Library, The Royal Society and The Linnean Society. The Victoria and Albert Museum also have a number of her original works.

How to make a cyanotype print

Materials:

- Ferric ammonium citrate 30g
- Potassium ferricyanide 15g
- 250ml water
- Paper, any size. A smooth watercolour paper or any absorbent substrate such as pale unvarnished wood, stones, cardboard etc. can be used. Natural fabrics also work well.
- Design elements of your choice like plants, stones or stencils.
- A bucket with seawater or tapwater.
- A lightproof bottle for storing photographic solution.
- A lightproof bag to fit your paper size. (both above available from photographic suppliers).

Method:

Mix the chemicals and the water in a measuring jug, then stir with a spoon. Use immediately or store in a lightproof bottle. This light sensitive solution will be enough to hand paint several sheets of paper and some fabric samples.

Use a sponge or acrylic brush to apply the solution to paper or fabric, use even strokes for an even surface. Fabric can be painted in the same way or submerged in a jug of solution (wear gloves).

Wring out the fabric and dry away from sunlight. It will turn the paper and fabric pale green. Store the completely dry paper and fabric in a lightproof bag until ready to use (this can be stored for up to a couple of months).

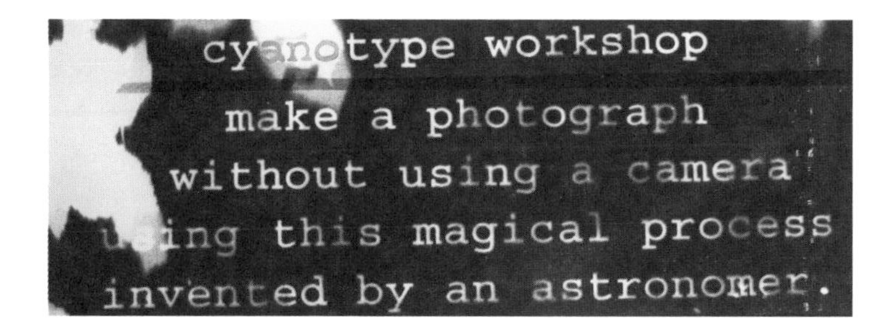

Place objects such as finely detailed plants, pebbles or elements of nature on to the green side of the paper or fabric…

…or drawings made in black lightproof ink or pen on tracing paper…

…or black and white acetate designs, printed from a reprographic centre or printer.

Pin or place glass over images if necessary to prevent any movement.

In summer sunshine the exposure time is 5 – 10 minutes.
On cloudy days, times will be longer… around 40 minutes.

Make test strips and note results according to season and weather patterns to develop knowledge of the process.

A UV lightbox or screen exposure unit can also be used where sunlight is insufficient.

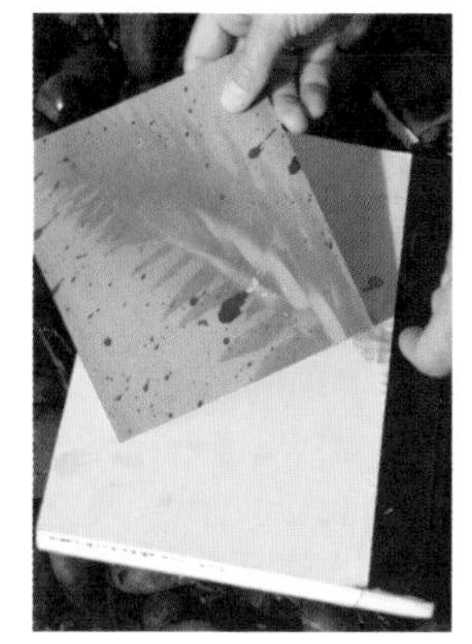

To fix the print:

The green paper will turn a greyish green when ready. Shake off the design elements and place the print in a bucket of cold water and gently agitate for one minute until all the chemcals are removed and the print turns blue and is fixed. Dry away from direct sunlight.

Perforated St. John's Wort

Scientific name: *Hypericum perforatum*

Flowers in the summer months from June to September.

Historically, the emerging red colour when the flowers were steeped in water led people to believe the plant had magical properties.

One folklore name is "chase devil." The plant was thought to keep evil spirits away when picked and dried on the solstice fire. Another name is "the herb of love". If kept in close contact to the heart it would attract love.

It is still used as a medicinal herb to treat depression and low moods.

Several species of Hypericum produce yellow and brown dyes. Only perforatum produces violet red shades, derived from the pigment hypericin.

The tops of the plants produce yellows.

Materials:

- As a rough guide use equal weight of flower heads to fabric.
- Dye pot and tongs.
- Water (enough to cover flowers and fabric with ample room to move.
- Clear vinegar.

Method:

Simmer the flowers until the dye liquid turns red, strain off the liquid. Add unmordanted wool or silk to the dye pot for shades of red and add a little clear vinegar.

St. John's Wort schnapps recipe

Pick a handful of flowers and add to a neutral spirit such as unflavoured vodka. Infuse for two weeks to allow the flavour and colour to develop. Strain through a coffee filter to separate flowers from liquid.

The red colour, symbolising love, can be used as a celebratory drink at summer weddings and sipped during sunsets. It will store well and can be enjoyed by the fire on long winter nights as well.

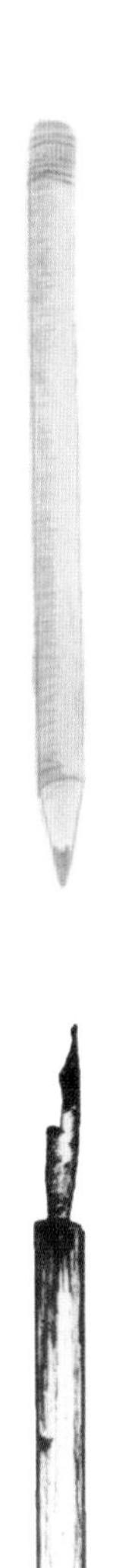

Autumn

Natural dyeing with Madder

Scientific name: *Rubia tinctorum*

Madder was one of the first dyes and evidence of the dye has been found on ancient Egyptian clothing and in Norse burial grounds.

Madder is a hardy perennial and was cultivated commercially throughout France, the Netherlands and southern Europe.

The colour from the plant resides in the roots which have various pigments, including alzarin red, yellow and brown.

The leaves are sprawling and tiny sharp spines on the stems can lacerate the skin, so handle with care when harvesting, and wear gloves. The roots need to be a pencil-width thickness and can take two to three years to grow from seed.

Materials:

- Madder roots
- Fabric (pre-mordanted, see page 91)
- Sieve or muslin
- Dye pot
- Tongs

Method:

Fresh or dried root is added to the dye pot, tie loosely in a muslin bag to prevent it becoming stuck to fibres.

Gently simmer, never boil.

Add fabrics to the dye pot, until desired colour is achieved.

As a guide use equal dry weight of dye roots to dry weight of fabrics for deeper shades.

An alum mordant will produce redder hues.

Many shades can be produced before the dye is exhausted. These colours include reds, oranges, salmon pinks to palest, delicate pinks.

Resulting colours depend on where the madder is grown, the soil type and when harvested. Make notes on the provenance of the madder, timings in the dye pot and fabric samples to extend your knowledge and to be able to repeat shades.

Exciting hues can be realised with different mordants and modifiers before and after the dye bath. See notes on iron water, page 59.

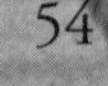

Natural Dyeing with Walnut

Scientific names: *Juglans regia, Juglans nigra*

The fallen green husks are used for dyeing purposes and give brown hues. Walnut leaves and bark also give shades of yellow and pinky tans. Soak the husks prior to dyeing for as long as possible. Adding a little clear vinegar can help prevent mould.

Staining is an issue – wear gloves, mind your hands and clothes.

Simmer a couple of handfuls of husks for one hour to extract colour.

Then add fibres and simmer or leave overnight to soak. Fabric can be re-dipped for darker shades. The husks can be re-used for further dyeing.

Modifying with iron water solution adds a range of darker colours – see page 59.

Dyeing with onion

Scientific name: *Alium cepa*

White onion skins produce a range of yellows and oranges.

Purple onion skins produce shades of green.

As a guide, use half the weight of dry onion skins to dry fabric weight.

No mordant is necessary.

A dyebath is a mixture of water and dye material. Both dyebaths can be modified afterwards and the colour palette extended with an iron water solution.

Iron water

To make iron water solution use a handful of rusty iron nails or discarded iron metal parts mixed with approximately one part clear vinegar and three parts water and leave for a couple of weeks in a labelled jam jar to rust.

Stir and take out spoonfuls of the solution to mix with water in a separate dye bowl to change the colours of fabrics by dipping them. Iron water solution will tone down and darken colours.

Alternatively, a couple of tablespoons of iron water solution can be added to the dyebath after dyeing. Rinse thoroughly and dry.

Lumen

Lumen photography is a way of creating beautiful photographic images without a camera.

You will need sunlight, inspiration and any 2D or 3D forms you are curious to see translated into a photographic image, such as silhouettes or botancial forms.

Materials and equipment:

- Black and white photographic paper and an extra lightproof bag.
- Glass or perspex to prevent movement of your design.
- Photograpic rapid fixer diluted with water as per supplier instructions.
- Two trays, one for the photographic fixer and one for water.
- Tongs, gloves and apron.
- Drying area for prints (washing line and pegs).

Method:

Plan your design layout.

In a blacked out space, open the box of photograpic paper and remove a few sheets. Store them in a second lightproof bag.

Due to the fact that photographic paper is light sensitive, this action will prevent your whole stock being exposed to light and destroyed.

Remove one sheet of photographic paper and place your design elements on the surface. Cover with glass or perspex on top to prevent movement if necessary.

Position outside in sunlight or by a window ledge. The longer the images are exposed, the more intensely the design is burned into the paper. This can range between minutes and days. Time for experimentation!

After your exposure, immerse your paper in the fixer for at least 30 seconds or for as long as suggested on the bottle.

Wash your print in water and hang to dry.

Once these prints are dry, you can paint over them using your botanical inks.

Winter

Botanical Inks

Long winter nights are perfect for using seasonally foraged and stored resources to make your field notes, journal pages and artwork from homemade inks.

Materials:

- Gum arabic solution – one teaspoon
- Organic thyme oil – a couple of drops
- Alum powder or crystals – one teaspoon
- Small cooking pot
- Any colour-yielding botanical matter, for example a handful of onion skins or soaked walnut husks.

Method:

Gently simmer your choice of colour-yielding botanical matter with water in a small pan.

Drain the liquid and save, discard the cooked botanical matter.

Reduce the liquid through further heating to intensify the colour.

Add the gum arabic solution to thicken and enable easy application.

Add the thyme oil to keep mould free.

What other plants can you explore to make a series of botanical inks? Your imagination is the limit.

The inks can be stored and labelled in old jars.

Devise mark-making implements from plant stalks or feathers to draw, paint and write.

Dyeing with botanical kitchen waste

Satsuma

Scientific name: *Citrus unshiu*

Discarded peel from several fruits can be soaked in water for a few days prior to dyeing.

Add some extra water and simmer gently in a dye pot for at least half an hour for delicate shades of yellow on silk and wool. Leave the fabrics to cool in the dye solution overnight to increase depth of colour.

Red cabbage

Scientific name: *Brassica oleracea*

Red cabbage contains a water soluble pigment called anthocyanin which changes colour when mixed with an acid (lemon juice or vinegar) or an alkali (baking powder).

Materials:

- Red cabbage
- Water
- Dye pot
- Heat source
- Tongs
- Lemon juice or clear vinegar

Method:

Add the red cabbage leaves whole or shredded to the dye pot, cover with water and simmer gently.

The liquid from the red cabbage is a mauve colour when heated with water.

Excitingly, lemon juice can be used to draw or paint onto the red cabbage dyed surfaces for vivid shades of pink.

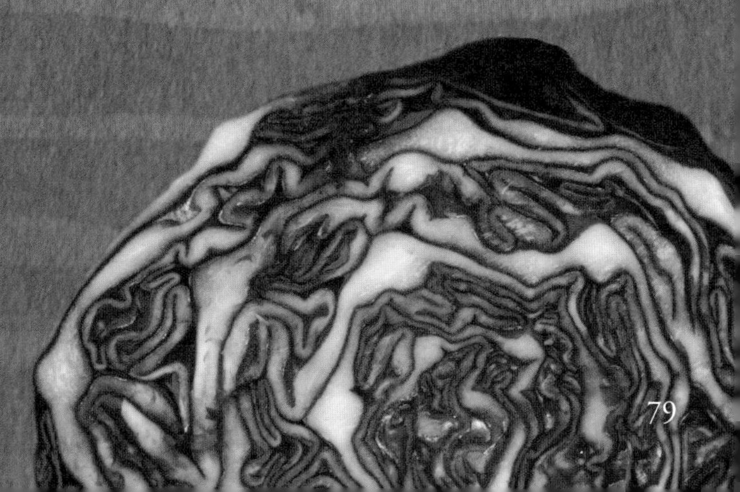

TOVE JANSSON The Listener

Browntoning

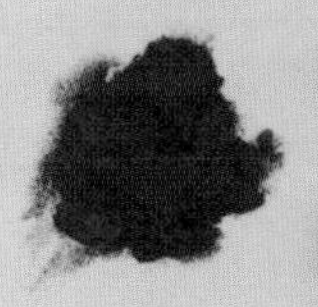

Method:

Turning cyanotypes/ blueprints yellow

Mix approximately one large tablespoon of sugar soap in warm water to dissolve crystals in a tray big enough to cover your paper size. Submerge the print and wait for the colour to change to yellow/tan. Wash the print in 2nd tray of tap water, use tongs and wear gloves.

Browntoning cyanotypes/ blueprints

First turn the cyanotype yellow as above, mix a tablespoon of tannic acid with warm water in a 3rd tray to make a paste and keep adding water until fully dissolved to cover print(s). Add the yellow prints to the tannic acid solution and submerge until required shade achieved.

Saved and used teabags (20+) can also be used to browntone.

Tannins can be found naturally in oak galls and the bark of many trees, simmer for an hour and allow to cool for a natural tannin solution.

Materials:

- Tongs, gloves and apron
- Water
- Sugar soap (DIY shop)
- Tannic acid or used teabags
- Three trays:
  – for sugar soap solution
  – for water rinse
  – for tannic acid solution

Basic Dyeing Equipment

- Dye Pot
- Tongs
- Scales for measuring dyestuff & fabric
- Access to water
- Heat source
- Apron - Gloves - Mask
- Fabric selection
- Fabric scissors
- pH papers

HEALTH & SAFETY WITH NATURAL DYEING

- Keep dyeing equipment exclusively for dyeing
- Handle any chemicals with care, some dyestuffs as well as mordants can be irritants or are toxic
- Ensure the work area is well ventilated and keep windows and doors open

MORDANTS

- Mordants help the fibres receive the colours and increase light and wash fastness.
- Aluminium sulphate is the most common mordant used for protein fibres such as wool and silk
- Tannin acts as a mordant and can be found in oak galls, bark, blackberry stems and staghorn summach leaves
- Rhubarb leaves, containing oxalyic acid, can also be used as a mordant
- Iron mordant can be made from any old iron soaked in water and a splash of clear vinegar and left to rust.